ALIVE AFTER CRISIS

A Comprehensive Guide For Emergency Planning and Crisis Survival

Richard Marshall

Table of Contents

A Disaster Scenario

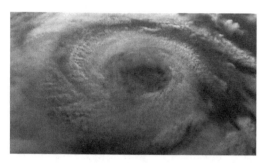

It's evening. The meteorologists have been predicting severe thunderstorms all day, over a huge swath of the country. In other states, where they're much more common, tornadoes have been reported. In your neighborhood, things are quiet, at least for now.

Your children are in the family room watch- ing TV when the community warning siren sounds. Your husband is not yet home from work, but you've rehearsed this drill with the kids before. You gather them up and you head for the base- ment. The dog is in the house somewhere; your son calls for him, but there's no response. You know—be- cause you prepared, and in preparing you learned it—that time is of the essence in these drills, so you don't wait. You close the door behind you as you head down the stairs.

Your designated shelter is the spare bedroom in the southwest corner of the basement. It has a bed and a couple of other pieces of furniture in it, plus some out-of-season clothes and spare blankets in the closet. Though you've been meaning to stock it with additional essentials, you haven't yet found the time. Still, there's a case of drinking water and a couple boxes of snack bars on the dresser, plus a flashlight on the nightstand. You don't know what became of the dual-powered clock radio that also used to sit there. You hand the flashlight to your daughter to hold. She clicks it on, then off. The battery is still good. You remem- ber, then, that in your haste you left your cell phone on the kitchen counter.

KA-CHUNK! KA-CHUNK! KA-CHUNK! KA-CHUNK!

It sounds at first like a locomotive off in the distance. You once heard someone who'd been through one use those very words in describing it, and that's exactly how it sounds. KA-CHUNK! KA-CHUNK! KA-CHUNK! KA- CHUNK! As it gets louder and closer, the pace of it quickens. Instinctively you move the children to the floor, between the wall and the bed, and you pull the comforter over the top of the three of you. The noise is now so loud and deep that it feels like it's physically hammering your chest. Your ears pop. You feel the foundation wall behind you shiver as the only window in the room, five feet above your head, shatters outward and the air in the room is sucked out. Further above you the house shrieks as it is torn apart, lifted, and crushed back downward violently. You close your eyes, you squeeze your children to you, and you pray.

Though it feels like it will last forever, you're surprised at how quickly it's over and completely quiet. The only sound you can hear now—besides the ringing in your ears—is the intermittent slapping of fat raindrops, hitting the living room floor directly above you. You can also hear your son's soft whimpers as he clings to you. Your daughter clutches you as well, but she is otherwise motionless and quiet. You lift yourself from beneath the comforter and discover that the room is now completely and impenetrably dark. By feel you retrieve the flashlight, still lying on the bed where your daughter left it, and with it you survey the room.

The ceiling and the walls look to remain solidly intact, though the door has been pushed in at the top, on the hinge side. You test it, and it will not budge. You also test the wall switch next to it, but it only tells you what you already know: no electric. The window and its frame are completely gone; the resultant naked opening just to the outside of it is entirely blocked by debris. It's the only other avenue of exit for you. Eerily, nothing else in the room has been damaged or disturbed in the slightest. None of you has physically suffered even a scratch. You sniff the air, and you detect no smell of gas or smoke. The beam of the flashlight begins to weaken, so you turn it off to save what power is left, and the three of you huddle together on the bed in total darkness. You resist the urge to call out for help. Save your energy, you recall being told. Stay calm. Don't panic. Go into survival mode. Best to just listen for now, you decide.

You understand that you are trapped in your shelter. The rainwater that you can hear dripping steadily in the interior corner tells you that the rest of your home, beyond this room, has undoubtedly been destroyed. You have no means of communicating with the outside world. It's night, and beyond your walls it's probably chaotic right now. Help from the outside world may well be many hours away.

You have a job to do. Of course you worry about your husband's fate. You worry that he's worrying about yours as well. You anguish over the dread that you feel in your children's

grips, the trauma you hear in their whispers. You ponder the days and the weeks and the months of hardship that lie ahead of you in rebuilding your lives. You wish that you had been better prepared. All of these thoughts weigh on you, but you also know— because you did prepare, and you learned it—that right now, sitting in the dark, you have a job to do.

Make it to next light. Make it until rescue finally arrives and the door is pushed free and light once again pours into the room. It may be tomorrow or it may be the day after that, but for now your plan is to simply make it that far. The rest of it will come later.

In these circumstances you can feel rightly confident that help will arrive sooner rather than later. You understand what you're going to need in order to hold out for that long: shelter, water, and food, in a safe and secure environment. You have assessed each of these, and you have concluded that, despite any deficiencies in your preparation, and with only a little creative adaptation, you can find it all right there with you in the room. Once you get beyond this crisis, there will surely be others for you and your family to prepare for and to survive; other moments of darkness with new and different challenges to overcome. Each of them will have a next light as well. What they will be doesn't matter to you right now, though. You have to make it to this one first. So do your job. Make it to next light. Survive.

It could be a tornado that wipes out your neighborhood, or it could be some other natural event of broader and more enduring impact, like a major flood or an earthquake. The disaster that impacts you could also be of the man-made variety, such as an act of terrorism or a global economic meltdown. It might arrive suddenly, altering your way of life overnight, or it might come to you gradually, over time, changing your world in fits and starts but always with a downward trajectory.

Just as likely, though, it will be a combination of more than one of these events converging at once, each on a less-than catastrophic scale, but with the sum-total result being far greater than the individual parts. A memorable example: Take a hurricane, add poorly-constructed public levees, an already-economically depressed area, and a failed government response and it equals New Orleans in 2005. More than one million people were permanently displaced by Hurricane Katrina, the largest population removal in U.S. history since the 1930's Dust Bowl. Disasters come in all shapes and sizes. For those impacted, the effects can last from a few days to forever. When disaster does occur, what matters most is not its cause, nor its scope or duration. What matters most for you and your family is how you deal with it; how you react to the new reality that you must face. That, in turn, depends on how well you have prepared for it.

This book is your trail map through the preparation process. In it you will learn a system for disaster preparation that focuses on your basic needs, and on what you must have in order to survive, regardless of the nature of the disaster that brings crisis to your doorstep. Whether you own a home or you rent an apartment; whether you are in an urbanized area or in a small community; whether you live alone or are the head of a family that depends on you to see them through difficult times, you will learn how to prepare for disaster—any disaster—before it happens, and how to survive it when it does.

Preparation of course includes the gathering of essential resources, such as shelter, water and food. That part of the process will be covered extensively here. However, before you begin you must first gather knowledge. After all, that is your most valuable resource. Throughout this book, an underlying theme that you will find is this: What you have available to you in a crisis is important to your survival; more important is what you do with it; more important than that is what you do without it. This is the knowledge that you must have before you can begin to prepare effectively.

The 1930's Dust Bowl

The 1930's Dust Bowl It is considered by many to be the worst disaster in U.S. history. Its causes were both natural and man- made. The lessons to be drawn from it are particularly resonant today.

Beginning in 1930, extreme drought came to this country. Over 75% of the nation was affected, but the southern plains states of Texas, Oklahoma, Kansas, Colorado, and New Mexico were hit especially hard. Though historically such weather events were a common, cyclical event in this area, the last previous such drought had been decades earlier. During the intervening years, unsustainable land use practices had been introduced and heavily employed, and as a result of too many years of over-planting and over-grazing, topsoil was left loose and depleted. With the drought came the winds. With the winds

came the dust storms. It lasted until the rains returned in 1939.

Over 150,000 square miles of southern plains farm land were rendered unfit for use for many years thereafter. An estimated 7,000 people died from lung diseases associated with the inhalation of dust. More than 2.5 million people fled from the affected areas. And all of this happened during the Great Depression. Other states such as California, already hobbled by their own economic hardships, were overwhelmed by the influx of refugees, and in many instances civil order broke down.

The most telling image of the Dust Bowl can be found in the monster storm that occurred in 1934. A massive dust cloud several miles across and two miles high, driven by 60 mile an hour winds, traveled from the Great Plains east across the country some 2,000 miles. On May 11, 1934 the massive cloud darkened the skies over Washington, D.C., as a gridlocked Congress debated a soil conservation bill.

I: What Is Preparation?

Disaster preparation starts with a basic understanding of survival, your most powerful instinct. When faced with something that immediately threatens your well-being, be it oncoming traffic, a charging bear, or a destructive tornado, your very core demands that you try to live through it. It's a part of your DNA; it's in your nature. When the threat is not so immediate, when it's a danger sensed but not yet within your sights, your rational mind takes over the job of coping with it, but the force driving you is exactly the same. So you prepare for it. Smart, competent preparation in advance of a crisis gives you a survival edge when that time comes. It's as simple as that.

Human beings have been preparing for expected disasters of one kind or another for as long as there have been human beings. In a sense everyone does it, every day, only on a more modest scale. If you buy a backup sump pump or you keep a box of candles in a drawer, it's not because you want to have to use them, or even that you expect to. You just want to be prepared. It's why Ben Franklin invented the lightning rod. It's why your car has a spare tire.

Even the seriously devoted modern-day "preppers," as they've come to be known, have been around forever. Noah was the first, though he had a distinct advantage over all those that followed: he knew exactly what was  coming. For everyone else, it's a day-to-day guess. You pay attention to the weather, and you follow local and world events, but you can never really know what to expect. You may have a sense of something, a disturbing uneasiness that this or that may disrupt your life some day, in some way, but you don't know what it will be. And what can you do about it today, before it happens? And what if you guess wrong? All you can be certain of is that you're not prepared for a drought if you've built yourself an ark.

The modern "prepping" movement is said to have begun in the 1970's, during that decade's oil embargo crisis, though hints of it can also be found earlier, in the Cold War atom bomb shelter era of the 50's and 60's. Since then, interest in disaster preparation as a serious pursuit has waxed and waned cyclically around other crises, real and imagined: Gulf War I, Y2K, 9/11 and the War on Terror, Gulf War II, Hurricane Katrina, the 2007 financial crisis, Hurricane Sandy, and the 2012 end of the Mayan calendar, to name just a few.

Interest in the "prepper" movement appears to be at its height today, and for reasons that are rather compelling. Droughts, heat waves, floods, and hellacious hurricane and tornado seasons foretell serious and troubling climate change consequences to come. The global economy has yet to recover from its 2007 collapse, and in some quarters it has actually gotten worse, as entire nations are imploding economically. In the U.S., unemployment and underemployment remain painfully high. Poverty is becoming more widespread. Our privatized prisons overflow. Gridlock stalls traditional government services, and austerity measures cut them back further. An aging infrastructure, both public and private, continues to crumble. Other than that, everything is just fine. If that disturbing uneasiness you feel just got a bit stronger, you are not alone.

II: Disasters Aplenty

Naturally, you might think that the first step in educating yourself in how to prepare wisely and competently would be to try to figure out what disasters are most likely to occur. Step two would then be to prepare for them. In truth, you can't possibly prepare for every potential disaster that might impact you. The numbers are just too staggering; the task is too daunting. The nature of the disasters that could occur can generally be categorized as follows, but even the seriously committed preppers don't all agree on this:

7 Nightmare Scenarios

1. **Major storm or other natural disaster:** This could be anything from localized flooding that lasts a few days, to an F5 tornado that wipes out an entire town, to a tsunami, to a Hurricane Katrina, to an eruption of the Yellowstone caldera. Theoretically, it could also include a major asteroid strike, with consequences too dire to even contemplate.

2. **Disruption of government services:** A police or fire (or highway or sanitation or health) department strike of some duration; or a substantial reduction in size, and therefore availability, due to budgetary constraints. It could also be the effective or actual shutting down of an entire state capitol for the same reason. Expand that notion to a service more national in scope, such as FEMA, and other consequences arise.

3. **Financial collapse:** Deep recession, hyperinflation, devaluation; a collapse of credit, and with it the housing market. In essence your money is no longer any good, so you can't buy food; but your grocer's money is no longer any good either, so the shelves are bare.

4. **Disruption or collapse of infrastructure:** Public or private, from widespread blackouts, to oil shortages or embargoes, to food or water distribution problems.

5. **War:** This includes insurrection and riot. It also includes acts of terrorism, which could result in a disaster that falls under one of the other categories. It also includes a prepper favorite, the electromagnetic pulse (EMP), a weapon-induced burst of electromagnetic energy that disables all electronic equipment within its range.

6. **Pandemic:** Avian flu, swine flu, or a resurgence of the black plague. Zombies?

7. **Complete societal collapse or other apocalyptic event:** Road warrior time.

To make it even more complicated, for each of these possibilities the severity can be measured in terms of:

● **Scope.** Is it localized or widespread?

● **Depth.** Is it the power grid only, or is it a complete cut-off of all goods, services, communications, and transportation?

Duration. Is it something that will last a few days, several months, or forever?

Each permutation presents a different set of problems. If the power grid is your only source of electricity and it goes down for a week in the summer, you can get by without air conditioning for that long. If it's a week in the winter, you'll have to figure out an alternative way to stay warm. If it's for the whole year, you'll have to either move somewhere else or be prepared to adapt to an entirely different lifestyle. How do you decide, then, which type of crisis you can reasonably foresee and therefore prepare against? The honest answer is: you can't. The planet is just too complicated. The potential problems, besides being too numerous to count, are also too unpredictable. You'd be guessing.

There is the allegory of the New Orleans resident who was an avid prepper. He read up on it, studied it, and taught himself survival skills. He filled the rafters of his house with extra drinking water, cooking fuel, and months' worth of food in anticipation of some world-wide catastrophe. When Katrina hit and washed his home away, he ended up in the cheap seats at the Astrodome with nothing but the clothes on his back, waiting to be rescued. He probably wished, in hindsight, that he had built himself an ark.

III: The Plan

If you cannot know, then how do you prepare? Where do you find your survival edge? You find it here, in a rational, knowledge-based plan that prepares you for any crisis. It does this by focusing not on the problems, but instead on a single solution. That solution begins by focusing on you, and on your most basic human needs. It looks to what you must do and what you invariably must have in order to survive any crisis. It is a simple, straightforward strategy that is suitable for both the beginner and the seasoned prepper who's in search of a better approach to preparation.

Generally, your most basic human needs are: shelter, water, and food, in a safe and secure environment. These are what you physically require in order to keep living. The next four chapters will cover each of these four components; they are your plan to survive. At the start of the second chapter, on Shelter, you will also learn more about why these are your basic human needs, and why this strategy of focusing on them works. In each chapter you will also learn practical steps for preparing yourself, and a variety of methods for finding or providing what you need in adverse conditions. In the final chapter, on a Safe and Secure Environment, you will find out what to do ahead of time to make your home a safer place to weather any storm, natural or man-made. You will also learn more on the basics of a survival strategy, particularly as it applies to dealing with circumstances that are an immediate threat to your well-being.

That is the ultimate survival challenge you can face; when your entire focus is to make it to next light.

IV: Attitude

Before getting into basic physical needs, however, let's take a look at your mental and emotional state. How best should you react to a crisis when it arrives? More specifically, where does your head need to be? The answer is, somewhere calm and focused. It's called the right attitude; its evil step-sister is called panic.

Scientists now know that every experience that a human being has, including every bit of sensory input received, must first pass through the portion of the brain that's responsible for the panic response. Before you can consciously think about it, the primitive part of your brain has to first tell you whether or not you need to run away from it. Or attack it. Or stand there like a mad person and scream yourself hoarse at it.

Panic is an ancient, natural, and incredibly powerful emotion. It's your most powerful instinct and a component of survival, but it was designed for the days of the savannahs, when fight-or-flight was the best defense against one's enemies and the mighty beasts. In a modern-day, real-life survival situation, it can be incredibly destructive. Once surrendered to, panic is nearly impossible to

Preparation: A Matter of Choices

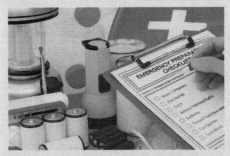

Preparation is not a contest to see who's right, or who turns out in the end to be the best prognosticator of what is to come. It's a matter of personal choices. Others can ignore everything that's going on in the world, or they can follow it all diligently and still choose to do nothing. But as you decide to move forward, there are a number of questions that you should ask yourself:

- Who am I doing this for? Is it for myself, or for myself and my family? Are my neighbors to be included in this? How about my friends or other relatives, or anyone else who I can expect to come knocking on my door if conditions get really bad? How about my extended community, perhaps as part of a more organized, concerted effort?

- How prepared do I want to be? Enough to last a week, or a month, or a year? Enough to withstand a severe weather event? Or the complete collapse of society as I know it?

- Do I go off-grid? How far? Do I make a plan to "bug out" for somewhere else when trouble arrives?

- Who do I share my plan with? Or do I keep it a secret?

Each question is a choice to be made. Each choice has consequences; you may never know what all those consequences will be, but the choices have to be made.

control. Wilderness survival experts teach that panic will kill you quicker than anything else in the wild; that the toughest terrain to negotiate out there can oftentimes be the distance between your ears.

The same holds true for the survival situations discussed in the coming chapters. Coping with the unexpected and dealing with dangerous conditions requires great ability to think calmly and with clarity, and to cleverly adapt to changing circumstances. That is the only attitude that works. Panic undermines that ability.

The strategies and the approaches suggested in the coming chapters are all based on the assumption that, when the situation is at its most threatening or difficult, you will be at your coolest. You have to be in order to survive.

Review of Chapter One

What have you learned in this Chapter?

- Disaster preparation means survival.

- You can't prepare for every potential disaster.

- Your most basic human needs are shelter, water, and food, in a safe and secure environment.

- The proper mental attitude is essential to survival.

- Preparation is a matter of choices.

What is your plan at this point?

1. Other topics to consider and to discuss with others:

2. What does the experience of being in a true survival situation feel like?

3. What types of disasters are most likely to impact your community, and how soon? What will be their scope, their depth, and their duration?

4. How well prepared are you for them right now, and what steps should you take to better prepare for them?

5. How do you control panic?

MODULE TWO SHELTER

I: The Rule of 3's, All 4 of Them

▸ **3 minutes—oxygen.** If you are deprived of oxygen for up to three minutes, you face imminent death.

▸ **3 hours—shelter.** If you are deprived of adequate shelter or other provision for warmth in cold conditions, in as little as three hours you will be hypothermic to the extent that it is life-threatening.

▸ **3 days—water.** If you are deprived of drinking water for up to three days, you will be dehydrated to the extent that it is life-threatening.

▸ **3 weeks—food.** If you are deprived of food for up to three weeks, you will suffer starvation to the extent that it is life-threatening.

The **Rule of 3's** is of unknown origin. Variations of it can be found in just about every outdoor survival guide ever written. As a rule, it isn't very rule-like. There are assumptions built into it, such as that the person it's being applied to is in relatively good health, and that the circumstances in 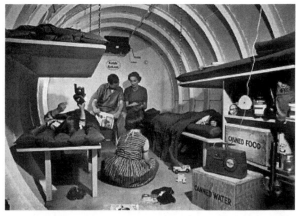 which it's applied aren't too extreme. Super athletes and the infirm don't count, nor do the middle of the Sahara or the North Pole.

The 3 minutes—oxygen part of the rule is hard and fast, but it's almost never discussed at length in any of the guidebooks, and for good reason. If you are in a survival situation—any survival situation—your access to breathable oxygen will hopefully not be an issue. If it is, there's not much advice anyone can give you, and not much time for you to remember it and act on it anyway.

The other three components of the rule—**shelter, water,** and **food**—are particularly unruly. Later in this Chapter, for instance, you will see that shelter includes a lot more than a roof over one's head, and sometimes it doesn't even include that. It's really more accurately described as the need for warmth. The time elements for all three of these are imprecise at best. Many survivors have been able to last more than three days without water; many more less. How long an individual can actually last without food depends on far too many factors to gauge precisely.

What these three components do provide, however, is an effective outline for a basic survival strategy. They do so at three different levels:

First, although the terms **shelter, water,** and **food** are by themselves too general to be very informative at the practical level, they really do describe, in simple terms, what human beings physically need in order to keep on living. Your ancestors were able to live and thrive in harsh wilderness for eons with nothing more than these three components. You can easily last two weeks snowbound in the family room with the same. So, when you are gathering resources as part of the preparation process, anything that is prepared, stored, and saved that effectively serves your needs for **shelter, water, and food** should be considered essential. Everything else is cotton candy.

Secondly, those imprecise time elements do serve to prioritize a person's needs in a crisis, by dictating the order in which they should be addressed. The three hour time frame for shelter is the shortest, so it must be considered first. Water comes next, then food.

Go back to the Scenario at the beginning of Chapter One. In that situation the mother, having learned all of this in advance, went through the very same process as she and her children sat trapped in the dark in the basement of their tornado-ravaged home. Observe how she hit every mark:

1. She calmed herself, and reminded herself not to panic.

2. She set her mind to survival mode.

3. She gave up her expectations, accepted her circumstances, and prepared to adapt.

4. She then assessed her essential needs.

As to shelter, it being the first of the three to assess, she observed that the room was intact and relatively weatherproof; she also knew that they had blankets and additional clothing to keep them adequately warmed, should cold arrive before rescue. As to water, and then food, she recognized that they had a good supply of each right there with them in the room; it wasn't a richly diverse supply, but it would suffice. She knew that they had everything essential they would need.

Putting it another way, she had a plan. That is the third level the Rule of 3's provides for a basic survival strategy. There are literally hundreds of stories written of amazing survival, from climbers trapped atop blizzard-swept mountain peaks to families trapped in their homes after a storm. These have been studied, and what has been learned from them is that the ones who make it typically do so because early on they came up with some kind of a plan to survive. It could be one that was based on years of professional training and rehearsal, as in the case of a seasoned alpinist or a veteran soldier, or it could simply be something half-baked and impromptu, that was hatched in the moment of crisis. But a plan to survive gave those who were affected a goal to work towards, a reason to keep trying and to keep living. Placing yourself in the proper frame of mind, and then assessing and providing for your essential needs, is a plan to keep living. With it, the nature of the crisis could be anything. The focus is instead on the solution. The crisis itself, whatever it might be, is the unfamiliar environment to which you must adapt.

II: Is it Shelter or is it Warmth?

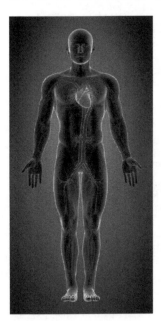

It's definitely warmth.

The basic biology behind it is not that hard to understand. You are a warm-blooded creature, so you need to maintain your body's core temperature within a narrow range in order to thrive. For homo sapiens, it's in the high nineties. If your body gets cold and your core temperature goes down just a little, you feel uncomfortably cold, and you put on a sweater. If it gets too cold, you feel very uncomfortable. You begin to shiver, and your body starts doing things like shutting down the blood flow to your extremities, in order to concentrate it more towards your vital organs.

Eventually, as you continue to lose body heat and your core temperature drops further, the shivering becomes sustained and uncontrollable. The blood flow to your brain begins to shut down, and you lose the ability to think coherently. You are now well into experiencing hypothermia, and if you don't act, it will kill you very quickly.

The human body is essentially a furnace. In doing its work, it produces the energy needed to maintain its core temperature in one way only: it burns what we eat. So we feed it. As it does its work, it produces and sheds spent energy in the form of heat. There is a reason why the ideal room temperature for humans is about seventy degrees, or almost thirty degrees cooler than the optimal core body temperature. That difference is just about right for shedding the excess warmth at just the right rate. At eighty degrees that process is slowed, and we begin to heat up; at sixty degrees the process becomes too fast, and we begin to get cold.

As to the other end of the thermometer. If your surrounding environment is too hot (think desert), so that your body is unable to effectively shed the excess heat it produces as it performs its bodily functions, then your core temperature will rise, and you will begin to experience what eventually becomes heat stroke, another potentially fatal condition. As with too-cold conditions, the problem here is also warmth, but in this case too much. Here, too, an actual physical shelter is merely one of the many options for dealing with it. More on that below.

III: Keeping Warm

There are essentially three different ways that you can either maintain your body warmth or restore it:

1. Crank up your internal furnace.

- Do some jumping jacks, since exercise increases the body's work load and therefore its heat production (but not so much that you perspire heavily, or you'll have the other problem of being wet). Experienced campers will often do some light calisthenics before turning in on a cold night, since the additional heat thereby produced helps warm up the inside of their sleeping bags more quickly. You do the same thing when you get out of your warm, comfortable bed on a cold morning, and you run to the shower instead of casually sauntering to it.

- Allowing yourself to shiver for a while also works, since that is simply the body's form of involuntary exercise (as long as it's not sustained and uncontrollable, which, remember, is an onset sign for hypothermia).

- Another option is to drink or eat something, not because it's necessarily additional fuel that immediately gets tossed into the hopper, but because the digestive process is work that the body performs, and that work produces more heat.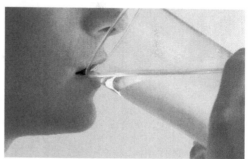

- While stimulants, such as caffeine and so-called fast-energy products, do artificially make you feel like things have sped up, in a true warmth-maintenance or recovery situation, that feeling won't be enough, and in the long run it could make the situation worse.

- Note once again that no shelter-building is required with this approach; also note, however, that it will not be sufficient, by itself, to solve a significant and sustained heat-loss problem. For that, you will need an external heat source.

2. Insulate.

- This is the most efficient means of maintaining the body's warmth. When you turn on the furnace in your home and heat it on a cold day, the insulation in the walls and above the ceiling helps to slow down the process of all that warmth basically leaking to the outside.

- Clothing does the same thing, but the furnace is inside of you and the room being heated by it is the thin layer of air between your skin and the material next to it. The right type and thickness of the material helps keep the heat from leaking out too rapidly. Wrap your entire house with an additional layer of insulation, and it becomes even more energy efficient, because your heat loss to the outside is further reduced and your furnace has to run even less. Put on more clothes, or wrap yourself in a blanket or a sleeping bag, and the same thing happens. How low can you go, outside temperature-wise, and still get by with nothing more than the heat that is being generated naturally, inside of you? They make sleeping bags that are industry- rated to -50ºF. And they work. In a crisis, enough of anything natural or man-made that can be layered and acts like insulation will do.

- Note here, too, that if the heat loss is significant and sustained, you will need an external heat source to remedy it.

Layering For Sustained Warmth

The most efficient way to keep warmth up is a space blanket. However, if not used properly, you could find yourself in an immense amount of trouble. Space blankets are most commonly packaged flatly folded up, which usually takes around 30 seconds to fully unfold. Unfortunately, the thin material will become as cold as the surrounding air in the amount of time it takes to unfold it so do not wrap it around your bare skin. Instead, use something to make a layer between you and the space blanket; such as a jacket or blanket. Also, keep in mind that only one side of space blanket is used to reflect radiated heat. If you are using one that has two silver sides, it will be the side that is slightly shinier. If you are using one that has two different colors on each side, the silver side is the correct side to use.

A thick down overcoat, filled with feathers or a fluffy synthetic material, keeps you warm in cold weather because inside all of that fill are millions of tiny little pockets of dead air space, and energy, particularly in the form of heat, has a hard time passing through dead air. It doesn't even need to be particularly warm air, so long as it's dead, or not circulating. A single, thick layer of down sometimes has its disadvantages,

however. If the fill is natural feathers, and they get wet, they tend to stick together and there go the air pockets. This can happen with the synthetic fill as well, if it is somehow compressed, such as from sitting on it. The other disadvantage is that all the insulation is in a single layer. If you start to get too *continued...*

- **Use an external heat source.**

- If in your house, turn up the furnace.

- Fill a hot water bottle and stick it in your pants.

- Drink some hot tea.

- Sit in the sun.

- Make a fire.

An external heat source can be utilized to maintain or to restore internal body warmth. Though it is by some measures the least effective of the three, in certain situations it will be not only the best choice, but the only one. Sometimes, when a person is so hypothermic that the body simply cannot recover sufficiently or quickly enough on its own, an external assist is the only viable option. Sometimes, despite everything you've tried, you just can't get your toes warmed, and it feels so good to stick them in a pan of hot water. Sometimes you get tired of huddling under all those blankets. Anyone who's stood in front of a blazing campfire, warming their hands as their backsides got colder, appreciates that these are not particularly efficient methods for obtaining warmth; a lot of it simply radiates away. Anyone who owns a fireplace knows that they can use up enormous amounts of resources. Anyone who's set down a cup of hot tea for just a

warm in it, besides feeling uncomfortable, you perspire. The sweat evaporates (even under your clothing), and that process of evaporation, when taking place on your skin, actually draws the heat out of you much faster than it would normally radiate on its own. Your only option,

That's why people who spend a lot of time active in the outdoors in cold weather dress in layers. If you are active and you feel warm, you take off a layer. If you feel cold, you put one or two back on.

Each layer, though thinner than a down coat, has its own tiny pockets of air, and between each layer is more dead air space, so cumulatively you end up with the same effect, but with many more heat- regulative options. And with the newer, lighter, synthetic materials, with their ultra sweat-wicking and moisture-blocking properties, you get even more. The currently recommended types of clothing and their order, for layering purposes, is as follows:

- **Base Layer.** This is what goes next to your skin. Before plastics, the underwear of choice for arctic explorers was silk. It's not particularly insular or durable, but it is comfortable and it does have the unique ability to move moisture away from body, outward to the next layer of clothing. Another choice that does the same thing is wool, which is warmer that silk, but it comes from sheep and, particularly when next to your skin, it never quite loses that identity. Today there are dozens of synthetic materials that add warmth, durability, moisture control, and even odor absorption properties, to their list of advantages.

continued...

minute, or sunned themselves on a warm spring day when suddenly the clouds rolled in, knows that they can be fickle. Still, all that said, human beings undeniably can't live without them.

At the end of this chapter is a list of items that should be considered when gathering resources as part of the preparation process. Included in that list are many products that directly relate to the topic of shelter/warmth as an essential need.

A final word about the other end of the thermometer. As you've seen, the human body is quite remarkable as a furnace. As an air conditioner, it's not all that great. You sweat; that's about it. In reality, the human body is almost entirely reliant on outside help of one kind or another in order to cool itself in too-warm conditions. Shade, a breeze, and inactivity help a lot. In sunlight a hat and lightweight, long-sleeved clothes covering do too. Lots of water is essential.

- **Mid Layers.** This is where the bulk of the layering occurs. The best choices here are wool sweaters or shirts, or any of the bulkier synthetics, like fleece and the poly-whatevers. In colder conditions down can also work here. These, too, all move moisture away from the body. The right number of layers depends on how many it takes to keep you feeling comfortably warm.

- **Outer or Shell Layer.** Here's where the truly amazing modern fabrics come in. Gone are the days of the rain gear make from greased animal skins or rubberized cloth. The best of these products are themselves layered concoctions that are thin and lightweight; rainproof, windproof, and breathable; they take a beating, and they look sharp for a long time.

Notice that cotton is never mentioned. It's a remarkably durable fabric that works great in warm conditions, primarily because it is extremely absorbent and it gives up the moisture it absorbs very slowly. If you need a lot of cooling, evaporative action next to your skin in, say, a desert environment, nothing beats a cotton T-shirt in a breeze. But those very same qualities render it useless or worse in cold weather conditions. When cotton is dry it's fine, but once it gets wet it stays wet, as its little pockets of air fill up with water and it loses its ability to insulate. You can use it as a towel or a bandana, but in cold weather conditions keep cotton out of your dress code.

IV: At Last, Shelter

Is your home essential to your survival? Well, yes and no. You could manage with much less, but as long as it remains structurally intact it will work wonderfully in providing most of your basic needs for shelter/warmth. If the power is off or the furnace is out, you may have to find alternative means for providing some warmth (fire in a fireplace or wood stove only; don't rely on a gas stove, it won't provide enough heat to outweigh the dangers of burning the place down), or be prepared to hunker down in a cold interior. Grab all the blankets, sleeping bags, and anything else that you can wrap yourself in. Even if the water is shut off (more on that in Chapter Three), your house is still your best option for shelter. It's where you live. If you have a better option readily available to you, go for it. Otherwise, stay put.

But even if your house is destroyed, you are by no means out of survival luck. There are many other options available:

- Friends

- Relatives

- Government temporary or emergency housing.

- In extreme conditions, a vacant house or building, or just about any other existing structure of some kind (so long as it is safe to be in it) should be your next choice. It's simply a lot easier to stay out of the weather and take care of yourself in one.

- On a temporary basis, your vehicle is another option. So is a tent in the backyard.

- When all else fails, adapt, build yourself a nice, warm Leaf Shelter, and set up housekeeping.

Shelter is about warmth. It is the first and most immediate of your basic human needs. Not every shelter necessarily provides you with a Safe and Secure Environment, however, and the two should not be confused. You'll learn more on this topic in Chapter Five.

Building an Emergency Leaf Shelter

After the first night in your Leaf Shelter you'll understand why it's considered to be the shelter of last resort. You won't sleep. You'll be stabbed by broken twigs, tickled by dead leaf material, and crawled on by bugs, and when you get out of it in the morning (you'll have no inclination to linger there), you'll be cold, tired and dirty, but you'll be alive. That's what a Leaf Shelter is supposed to do, keep you alive, and it does it better than any other natural-materials shelter that you can build. With enough attention to it, it can adequately shelter you in wet conditions to well below freezing, for weeks or even months, if necessary.

It takes a lot of time (several hours at least), energy, and materials to build one. If it rains the first night, besides being cold, you'll most likely get wet, so on that second day you'll have to spend more time and energy, and find more materials, to beef it up. You will never get it perfect on the first try. If on the second night you actually fall asleep, it'll probably be because you're simply too exhausted and you can't stop yourself. But again, the next morning you'll still be alive. After that, you'll start thinking of it as home. Like any home, it will have its maintenance issues, but like any home, you'll soon start to think of it as yours. That attitude, too, will help to keep you alive.

It's certainly possible to survive with a well-constructed Leaf Shelter long enough to put together or find something more traditional and friendly, or to be rescued. An important objective to keep in mind is that you are building yourself a sleeping bag more than a tent. Yes, it does have a somewhat rigid frame to it, and it does keep the wind and rain off of you, like a tent does, but more importantly the leaf litter, dead grasses, and other materials from the forest floor that make up the bulk of it are what you are going to wrap yourself in, like a sleeping bag, to keep yourself warm. A lean-to or any of a dozen other types of natural-materials shelters can also protect you from the elements like a tent does, and with the addition of a fire pit can provide you with an external source for warmth, but they will not keep you warm—that is, insulate you from internal heat loss—the way a Leaf Shelter does.

1. Start with a long, heavy, fairly straight dead branch, about the thickness of your wrist and 1 1/2 times your height in length. Prop up one end of it in a tree notch or on a rock or deadfall that's about hip high, and leave the other end of it (preferably the thinner end) on the ground.

2. Gather as many finger-thick dead branches as you can find, from shin to waist high in length, and lean them all against and up to the top of the pole (but not too much beyond the top),

continued...

densely, all along its length, all at about the same 45 degree angle. Be sure to leave an opening at the front (the higher end) for an entryway. These are the walls. If you can find some long, sinewy branches or lengths of vine (watch out for poison ivy), you can weave these through the leaning wall branches to give them better strength and stability. You now have your Leaf Shelter frame.

3. Now to the hard part. Gather every scrap of loose forest floor litter that you can find. Depending on the time of year, you may well have to scour far and wide. Wet litter will work fine, so long as it is not matted and decomposing, but dryer is better. You can lay a tarp or a blanket, or even your jacket or a shirt on the ground and sweep the litter onto it with your hands, to make carrying and transporting the stuff more efficient.

4. Throw all of this material on top of the frame, loosely, and keep doing this until the entire length of the frame is covered to a depth that, if you reach into it and touch the center pole, covers your entire arm up to your armpit. Done right, when you are finished, this will keep you dry and warm down to 32 degrees; if it also covers your torso and the far shoulder, you'll be good down to zero (good being a relative term here).

5. Not finished yet. Gather even more litter and start filling up the interior of the shelter. Jam it full. When this is done, climb in, feet first (always feet first), and squirm around, crushing the materials. Then crawl out and go get some more litter, and fill it up again. Crawl back in and squirm around. Do this three times, but after the third fill-up, when you crawl inside, stay there for the night. If you have a sleeping bag or a blanket (including a space blanket), wrap yourself in it first, before crawling in. It will keep you warmer and dryer, and it will also cut down on the twig stabs and the crawly things.

This is a one, or at most two-person shelter (and that other person better be somebody special, or both of you will need to be incredibly adaptive and tolerant). For a larger group, each person will have to build his or her own, which will necessitate ranging even farther and wider to find enough materials.

Obviously, this only works on high, dry ground in a forested or deep prairie setting. Even

there, it's a lot harder to find sufficient materials in the spring than in, say, the late summer or fall. In the desert, it can be very difficult to find sufficient materials; in an urban setting (security concerns aside for now) it's possible, but you'll have to be creative in finding enough man-made materials to do the same job as forest litter. In the winter, if there is any significant depth of snow cover, it simply can't be done, and you should carefully re-think the survival strategy that brought you there, at that time of year, in the first place.

Review of Chapter Two

What have you learned in this Chapter?

- The Rule of 3's: Oxygen, 3 minutes; shelter, three hours; water, three days; food, three weeks.

- The Rule of 3's provides a basic survival strategy.

- Shelter, which is really warmth, is the first priority.

- Hypothermia can be a serious problem in as little as three hours.

- The three ways to keep warm are: Crank up the internal furnace, insulate, and use an external heat source.

- So long as it is intact, your home is the best option for shelter.

What is your plan at this point?

1. Other topics to consider and to discuss with others:

2. What are the signs of hypothermia?

3. What types of clothing provide the best layering, and in what order?

3. How well prepared are you to provide for warmth within your home if your usual heating source is unavailable?

List of Items for Preparation

1. Wood burning stove and fire-starting materials.

2. Wool and synthetic clothing for layering.

3. Rain gear.

4. Sleeping bags and blankets.

5. Space blankets.

6. Tent.

MODULE THREE
WATER

I: Dehydration

You have now calmed yourself, you are not panicked, and your mindset is in survival mode. You've taken an immediate assessment of your basic human needs, those being **shelter, water,** and **food.** You have already considered your situation as far as shelter is concerned (which, as you've learned, is really more about warmth), and you have determined that you've done what you need to do to in order to take care of it for now. Next is water.

According to the **Rule of 3's**, if you go up to three days without drinking water you will die. It's as simple as that. It's called dehydration, and it's a terrible way to go. Even in its early stages—which can actually begin as soon as within an hour, depending on your activities and your environment—it's no fun.

Dehydration is a progressively debilitating and painful condition. In its early stages its symptoms can include:

● Dry mouth.

● Infrequent, dark-colored urination.

● Lethargy and fatigue.

● Muscle weakness and cramping, including stomach cramps.

● Headache and dizziness.

● Confusion and short-term memory loss.

- Sudden anger or other mood swings.

Its later stages can bring on:

- Absence of sweating when it should be expected.

- Increased heartbeat and lowered blood pressure.

- Delirium.

The final stage is unconsciousness, followed quickly by death.

The cure for dehydration is water. Lots of it. Once you are into its later stages, the curative process of re-hydration can require several days of serious fluid-pounding and rest. In the final stage, urgent intravenous medical treatment is required to prevent death.

You can readily see that, even in its early stages, dehydration can seriously compromise your ability to think clearly, and therefore your ability to cope effectively with the challenges of a crisis. The three days part of the rule for water provides you with an absolute, outside parameter only. It assumes that you are starting out hydrated; that you are average sized and in reasonably good health; that you are in a temperate (not-too hot and not-too cold) environment; and that you are not engaged in any particularly strenuous or stressful activities. In a crisis situation, however, you can't afford to wait that long.

II: How Much Water?

Once again, the biology of human water consumption is pretty basic. Your body is about 75% water. You need to regularly take in water, because your body requires a lot of it in order to function properly, and you're constantly giving it up. A human being typically loses the most water through respiration, perspiration, and urination. What you give up you need to replace. How much depends on a lot of factors, but the most important ones are generally:

- Your size

- Your health

- Your environment

- Your activities

It gets complicated, and there is a lot of conflicting information out there, but the following general guidelines should be helpful:

For a person of average size who is in reasonably good health and is not in an extreme environment, or engaged in strenuous or stressful activity, it is 2 liters per day, or about eight 8-ounce glasses. That seems to work as a safe minimum. Besides body size (bigger means more, smaller doesn't necessarily mean less) and health (cold or flu means more; a serious health issue, such as significant blood loss, vomiting, or diarrhea, means much, much more and is far too complicated to deal with here), any one—or any combination—of the following factors will increase that minimum:

- **Cold weather.** Outdoors, in below-freezing temperatures, your body can lose an additional 1-2 liters per day through respiration alone. Can you see your breath? That's water.

- **Hot weather.** With just moderate activity, you can lose an additional liter per hour through perspiration alone.

- **High altitude.** With only moderate activity you can lose an additional 1 liter per hour through respiration alone.

Activity. Whatever the environment, the more strenuous the activity, the greater the water loss, mostly through respiration and perspiration. Even at normal temperature and altitude, this can be as much as an additional liter per hour. In a more extreme environment this, too, gets multiplied. For example, with strenuous activity in very hot conditions (say, wrestling with a sand-stuck tire in the middle of the desert) an average-sized person can sweat a gallon in less than an hour. That is enough fluid loss, by itself, if not quickly replaced, to bring on serious, later-stage dehydration.

Digestion. If you eat a big meal of solid foods, you'd better drink a lot of water, because your body is going to use up a lot in processing it.

The best gauge for how much water you personally should be taking in is your own body. If you feel thirsty, drink. If you're peeing dark yellow, or you're getting a headache, drink even more, since you're probably already past the time when you should have. Better still, drink regularly and keep track of how much you are taking in, before any of these signs appear.

III: What Counts?

Good news for coffee and soda pop lovers: they count. So do teas, juices, milk, and other liquid, water- based libations, but with these caveats:

- Alcoholic drinks do not count. The body uses up a lot of water metabolizing alcohol.

- Coffee and some teas can have a diuretic effect (increasing the flow of urine) in some people, so it may not count 100%, though this is more likely to occur with the rookie latte sipper than with the seasoned, joe-swigging veteran.

- As with any liquid that contains more than just water (such as sugars or fats, as with soda or milk), the body has to process those extras, and that process uses up water, so you will need to drink more.

The water found in or added to the foods you eat, especially fruits, vegetables, and pasta, also counts, but with the same last caveat. If you feel hungry and all you have available is water, drink it; it will help. If you are dehydrated and all you have is a juicy tomato, absolutely eat it; if all you have is a saltine cracker, maybe not.

A word about salt. You do need it, and you expel small amounts of it in your perspiration and urine. Ordinarily that salt is more than adequately replaced through normal food intake. If not, some moderate salt loss, short-term (say a day or two), should not be a serious problem. Longer term—or even short term in very dry, hot conditions in which large quantities of water are being consumed and expelled and the salt loss is therefore rapid and significant—the salt deficiency can lead to a condition called hyponatremia, or water intoxication. The symptoms are similar to dehydration, except that you pee a lot and everything cramps up. The cure is simple: have something salty. If you don't have a saltine cracker handy, suck on that white crust that's formed on the sweatband of your baseball cap. It's salt.

IV: Conservation and Re-Use

Obviously, water is a most valuable resource in a crisis situation. Shelter is still your first concern, but with just a little advance preparation and some creative problem solving afterwards, any deficiencies can be taken care of relatively easily. With water, it's a different story. It's either there and available for you or it isn't, and no amount of advance preparation can guarantee that there will be enough of it when you need it. Without it, you're sunk. In a crisis, you have to quickly learn the art of conserving this most precious commodity. Better still, learn it and practice it (at least a few times) in advance. You can start by creating a water-cycling plan for your home.

The number-one priority use for the water you have available to you in a disaster is, of course, pouring it down your throat. What's at the bottom of the list? Things like filling the swimming pool, washing the car, watering the lawn, long lazy showers, and—yes, fairly far down there with these other trivialities— the toilet. If your home water supply is still functioning, and you're confident that it will remain so, go ahead and keep flushing away. If it isn't, or you have any doubts, number one and number two will have to be dealt with differently, because flushing them away uses up a lot of water.

This is not to say that that you necessarily have to construct an out-building with a crescent moon on the door somewhere in the back yard. In other places where water shortages are severe or water treatment options are limited, a common practice is to cycle the use of water through different stages. A typical cycle works as follows:

- Treated water is used for drinking and cooking purposes only.

- Clean but untreated water is used for washing dishes, bathing, and washing hands (always with plenty of soap; dishes can be rinsed with treated water if you wish, or be thoroughly wiped dry).

- The water used in these tasks is saved, and is in turn used for other tasks, such as laundry and general cleaning.

- That water is also saved, and it is used for toilet flushing. Dirty, brackish, untreatable water that you have access to can also be used by the bucketful for this purpose. Pour it in there as needed.

In a crisis situation, a swimming pool full of chemically-treated water can never be filtered or boiled enough to be suitable for drinking, but it is perfectly suitable for these other, secondary uses. Keep the cover on it to reduce evaporation, but also allow it to collect water when it rains. Once it's empty, if your access to other secondary-use water is limited, the door with the crescent moon on it should swing to the outside of the structure. Build it downwind.

Your ability to maintain a supply of fresh, clean drinking water is imperative to your survival, so don't take it lightly. You can learn the proper way to stockpile clean water, which filters are best to use and which ones will leave you sick from bacteria, how to decontaminate almost ANY water source, and many more life-saving skills in my Water Crisis Survival System. This book is available to Alive After Crisis customers only at a massive discount, so pick it up today at: http://aliveaftercrisis.com/flow/ water-crisis-survival-system/2/

Review of Chapter Three

● **What have you learned in this Chapter?**

● Water is the second priority, after shelter.

● You can go without water for at most 3 days before dehydration is life-threatening.

● You require 2 liters of water per day minimum.

● If there is any concern, TREAT IT.

● Rain is the safest source for natural water; lakes' rivers and streams are not safe.

● Boiling is the easiest method for treating water; filtering is the most effective way.

● Cycling water use preserves it

What is your plan at this point?

Other topics to consider and to discuss with others:

1 What are the signs of dehydration?

2. What sources of fresh water are available to you in your home or nearby?

3. What means do you have available to you for treating water?

List of Items for Preparation

1. 5-gallon bottles of purified water.

2. Durable, refillable water bottles and containers.

3. Private well hand pump.

4. Rain barrels.

5. Gravity-fed water filtration system.

6. Portable water filters.

7. Iodine tablets.

MODULE FOUR
FOOD

I: What's for Lunch?

Food is the third of the basic, human needs to be assessed in implementing your survival plan. You've already taken care of your shelter and water needs, so you have some time now, since the Rule of 3's tells you that it will take you another three weeks to starve to death.

When the shelves of the entomology section at your local grocery store are bare, you need only walk out to your own backyard—certainly no further than the nearest park or forest preserve—to find a fine, savory, plentiful selection of tasty little critters to choose from. In fact, there are well over a thousand edible varieties of insects to choose from in North America alone. Skewered, sautéed, fried, or even raw, in larva stage or legged, they are rich in nutrients and sure to please the palate of any hungry survivalist.

If you find the thought of eating bugs disgusting, then preparing for a long-term food shortage will be critical to your survival plan.

II: Starvation

Of all of the Rule of 3's time periods, the three weeks for food is the most wildly generalized. Many people routinely practice deliberate fasting (water only) for weeks-long periods at a time, with little or no deleterious effects. The longest reported time a human being has involuntarily gone without food and survived is somewhere in the 40-50 day range. Others have claimed even longer. On the other hand, particularly where conditions were harsh and stressful, people have been known to starve to death in under two weeks.

Complete fasting can also present more immediate problems for someone in a survival situation, because the process of slowly withering away typically becomes so debilitating so quickly—sometimes after only a few days—that the ability to think clearly and to carry out even the most basic tasks is severely compromised long before death ensues. And yet people have been known to function and last for months and even years with only the tiniest amounts of what barely qualifies as food, rationed and spread out over time.

The process of starvation, like that of dehydration, is gruesome and painful, but with starvation it takes a lot longer. During the first few days, the headaches, hunger pangs and cramping are bothersome but not crippling, as the body's metabolism slows down. After two days simple physical activity becomes more difficult and exhausting. On the third day of fasting, vivid dreams and a sense of great clarity of thought may be experienced; that is, in fact, the goal of the Native Americans' practice of the Vision Quest. After a few more days, the body, starved for calories and nutrients, begins to eat itself. Eventually it begins consuming its own vital organs, which then stop working. If you're ever in a situation where food is scarce, you may find yourself saying, "Pass the bugs, please."

III: How Much?

Reliable assessments of food distribution and supply networks calculate that there is no more than a two or three day supply of food readily available to the public at any given time. In a disaster, when local transportation and commerce are interrupted and people are in panic mode (witness the days following Hurricane Katrina), grocery store shelves can run empty in hours. In that situation, unless you

can get to another place that is not so afflicted, every one of your next meals will have to come from what you already have stored in your pantry, or what you are growing on your own. What's available in the wild will be strictly the province of those who know what they are doing out there.Obviously, then, storage becomes your best choice for anticipating a crisis. How much food and what kind, and how and where to store it, are your primary concerns.

How much depends on how many people you expect to be feeding, and who they are. Without getting into special dietary or other health needs, or too deeply into the optimal mix of dietary components (carbohydrates, fat, protein, minerals, etc.), suffice it to say that caloric intake is the most important metric here. It measures the amount of fuel that will be available for the body's furnace. What foods you choose to provide those calories with is up to you, so long as the calories are there in sufficient quantity to keep the furnace going.

How many calories are needed depends on each individual's age, gender, height, weight, and anticipated level of daily activity. There are charts and calculators widely available to help you in determining all of this, for example, www.healthycalculators. com/calories-intake-requirement.php. What they tell you is that a person's daily caloric intake requirements can range dramatically:

1. A petite, inactive, 60 year old female requires about 1,250 calories a day.

2. A 5'2", 110 lbs, fairly active 25 year old female requires about 1,700 calories a day.

3. A 6'2", 190 lbs very active 25 year old male requires 3,400 calories per day. If he's active out in the cold all day, make it 4,000. That's the equivalent of about 8 pounds of spaghetti with meat sauce that he will need to consume for one day.

Don't be surprised if you don't hit your recommended daily intake now and then. You will have to do the arithmetic, there's no getting around it. You will have to determine the caloric values for every type of food you choose to stock up on, and then add them up. If you also choose to pay attention to nutritional values, and things like good carbs vs. bad, it will mean more arithmetic. You may want to consider getting yourself a solar powered calculator and hope that it's EMP proof.

Then you will have to decide for how long you intend to feed yourself and this crew of yours. More choices, more math. A week? A month? A year? Stored food takes up a lot of space, and gathering it requires a lot of continuing investment, in terms of both time and resources. And homework. The magnitude of the task does not become apparent until you actually take it on. You will have to do that as well.

IV: What Kind?

For long-term storage purposes, fresh produce and dairy products—beyond the few days' supply that you might ordinarily have on hand anyway—are out. No more salads. The same applies to fresh meats, unless you have plenty of freezer/refrigerator capacity that will continue to work from a reliable alternative power source (such as a generator; propane and natural gas-powered freezers are also available). Barring such good fortune, expect that your supply of fresh meats will soon be gone. If you are a hunter or a fisherman with realistic access to game, and you know how to prepare and preserve it, blessings on you.

Non-perishable foods are the only realistic choice for most people's long-term, pre-crisis storage, with "non-perishable" being a relative term here. Everything has a shelf life. Check them. Once you start storing, get used to paying attention to such things, and to rotating your supplies from storage to the dinner table, or you will end up, over time, tossing out a lot of it.

Canned goods usually last a long time beyond their listed freshness dates. So do raw pastas. Rice is a great choice, since it is high in caloric content, can be easily stored by the bag, and can last for years when stored properly.Storage-wise, the same is true of sugar, salt, and coffee. Honey never goes bad. Flour (or things like cake mixes that contain flour) can be stored, but can go flat after only a few months. A better alternative might be un-ground wheat, which can be stored for years; you'll need a milling stone, too. Dehydrated foods are also a good choice so long as they don't call for the addition of a perishable item like milk or butter in order to prepare them, and they will last a long time in storage. This can include not just entrees, but also fruits and other favorites that may not be available fresh in a crisis. Second only to rice, nuts are also a great choice, in terms of both nutritional value and longevity. Nutritionally, after nuts come— seriously— insect larvae; they don't store well, however.

There are many other foods, plus herbs, spices, and other flavor additives that will last a long time when stored properly, and will give you many more options for preparing interesting meals. You can even take the next step and get into preserving, canning, freeze-drying and vacuum-sealing your own foods. The point here is to not starve in a crisis, but there's no reason why you can't make feeding yourself and your loved ones a little more pleasant in your unpleasant circumstances.

V: How and Where to Store

Bag it, then bag it again, then container it and keep it in a cool, dark, dry place. There are really no other secrets to storing food long term. Sunlight is an enemy. So are heat, moisture, and insects.

Be prepared to buy lots of heavy plastic food bags and big, durable, stackable plastic containers, the kind with a solid lid that snaps closed tightly—or better yet, water-tightly. Mark the contents, the storage date, and the expiration date of each item on the outside of each layer of containment. Keep a separate, written inventory for all of this information, and update it whenever you cycle foods into or out of the system.

If the product comes already sealed in an airtight container, say a 50 pound plastic bag of rice, that bag will count as the first layer. Anything less airtight than that, bag it twice before putting it in the container. Tape or tie-twist each bag tightly closed. If something is purchased in bulk, say in a corrugated box with a dozen individually-wrapped items inside of it, get rid of the box first and bag the individual items. Some bugs like that cardboard, sometimes even before it leaves the store.

Cool does not mean cold or hot, so storing the containers out of doors is not an option; neither is in an unfinished attic. A basement or crawlspace, provided it is within the weatherized envelope of the living space and is not prone to flooding, dampness, or mold, is an ideal location. Other choices would be a storage area under an interior stairway or a walk-in pantry. As a final option, be prepared to dedicate the closet in the spare bedroom—or if you'll also be feeding a few 25 year old male athletes, the entire room.

As with everything else covered in this book, making smart choices when assessing and attending to your needs for food is an important component of the preparation process. So is doing your homework. There are hundreds of sources available for more information on this; they can be found in your library, in your bookstore, and online.

VI: Where the Wild Things Grow

Finally, lest we forget, there is also Mother Nature and her rich bounty. If you are a gardener, then blessings on you as well, particularly if you are one who is so dedicated and skilled that you not only can harvest throughout the year, but you also can tell the difference between kale and the weeds surrounding it during its first week of growth. May you know only fruitfulness in your endeavors. If there is one skill that a beginning disaster preparer should learn and practice right from the outset, it's the art of gardening. When all else fails, Mother will provide.

There is her own garden to consider as well. Given enough wild, open space, either for you alone or shared with a limited number of other people of like mind and knowledge, it is certainly more than possible for you to live off the land and never want for a meal. Your hunter-gatherer ancestors did it for millennia, and enough of them lived lives that were healthy and productive enough to eventually produce you.

Being able to live off the land successfully, however, is not a skill that can be learned from reading a book or two. In fact, it can only be learned from years of practice and study. Among the ancients, one of the reasons the elders were revered in their communities was because of their knowledge of what to safely forage, where to find it, and when. The fact that they were still around in their golden years to impart this wisdom was the only measurement of their skill and success that was needed. Their educations began early in childhood. The ones who were no good at it—and didn't quickly switch majors—tended to achieve decisive failure early on (often only once), and were soon gone, either poisoned, starved, or banished for ineptitude.

For anyone raised in today's grocery market culture, if you're old enough to drink a beer as you read this book, then it is probably too late for you to begin your foraging education and expect to live long enough to get really good at it. And when it comes to edible plants, a little knowledge is often-times more dangerous than none at all. For just about every wild plant that you think you can identify on sight as being good for you, there's another that looks an awful lot like it that is toxic. For every part of that plant that you think you know to be edible—the fruit, the leaves, the roots—there's another part of it that will kill you. For every season in which it can be safely ingested, there's another in which you must avoid it. It takes a lifetime to learn all of these things.

That is not to say that the natural world should be completely ignored as a source for food in a crisis situation. Even a modest amount of self-education and field study can end up being well worth the effort, particularly if it comes down to a choice between eating something and going hungry. As an alternative to a career in botany, instead take the time to learn as much as you can about just a few plants. Choose one to begin with, something common to your area, and really get to know it: each part of it, by sight, touch and smell (not taste, not yet), at every stage of its growth and dormancy throughout the year (or two, in the case of biennials). Consult several field guides on it and learn about its look-alikes. Read up on its edible characteristics (it may have medicinal properties as well, which could also be valuable information in an emergency), and how best to harvest, prepare, and serve it. Do all of this until you feel confident that you know it as surely as you know an apple when you pick one up. Then, and only then, should you taste it.

Wild edibles can't be eaten in bulk, so don't expect to sit down whenever you want to and fill your belly. Most are best eaten by the nibble. In an emergency, however, a mouthful of fresh sheep sorrel or a couple of wild carrots can help stave off hunger pains, or as a side dish can help liven up an otherwise dull meal. Combined, two or three good choices can even become that salad you've been craving.

A good, easy first choice would be either the cattail, found in wetlands, or plantain, a ubiquitous broadleaf plant found along pathways and in untended lawns. Another good choice would be the all-too-familiar dandelion, all parts of which are both edible and highly nutritious. Good foraging, and blessings on you.

VII: Meal Preparation Cooking

There are many ways to make a tasty, hot meal for your family, even when your gas and electricity are out. The first and most obvious choice is to build a fire pit in your back yard and use that, although this process is a bit time consuming. Start by digging up a small hole in the shape of a circle about three feet in diameter, then lay stones around the edge. Gather small twigs and dry grass, if available, and set them in the middle. Using a lighter or matches, light the twigs to create a small flame. Once this is done you can add larger pieces of wood until you have a full size fire, but take care to stack the wood in a fashion that keeps it from falling outside of the fire pit as it burns. Now you can cook canned foods directly over the fire, or use cast-iron pots, pans, and skillets to prepare your favorite meals.

Another option is to use Sterno Cooking Fuel. These small, portable cans contain an ethanol gel which produces heat when opened and exposed to oxygen. Each can is good for about 2 hours of cook time, which should be sufficient for almost any emergency meal. While your long-term survival plan shouldn't rely on it, a supply of Sterno cans will make a short-term crisis easier to endure as you wait for the utilities to come back on.

A longer-term solution for daytime cooking is a solar oven. These work by reflecting the sun's heat into a confined space, usually a dutch oven, increasing the temperature in the center. These ovens are perfect for baking bread and cakes, as well as slow-cooking meats and vegetables, in a manner similar to using a Crockpot. You can learn how to build your own solar oven in Overnight Home Energy: A Comprehensive Guide for Going Off-Grid With a Self-Sustainable Power System, available at http:// aliveaftercrisis. com/members/

Review of Chapter Four

What have you learned in this Chapter?

● Food is the third priority, after shelter and water.

● You can go without food for about 3 weeks before starvation is life- threatening.

● How many calories you require per day depends on your age, gender, height, weight, and anticipated level of daily activity.

● Non-perishable foods are the best choice for long-term storage.

● Gardening is an important aspect of preparation.

2. What is your plan at this point?

Other topics to consider and to discuss with others:

1. How does short-term fasting affect you and your ability to function?

2. Which foods would you prefer to store in large quantity?

3. What wild edible plants are you familiar with?

List of Items for Preparation

1. Canned goods and other packaged non-perishables.

2. Rice and other grains.

3. Nuts and dehydrated foods.

4. Food-grade plastic bags.

5. Large, stackable, food-grade plastic containers.

6. Cooking and eating utensils.

7. Portable stove with butane or Sterno Cooking Fuel.

8. Milling stone and food-preserving equipment.

MODULE FIVE
A SAFE AND SECURE
ENVIRONMENT

I: Is it Safe?

Once your immediate needs of shelter, water, and food have been taken care of, it's time to ensure that you're in a safe and secure environment. Of the four basic human needs, this is the most difficult one by far. There is no Rule of 3's for it, so there is no time frame with which to prioritize it. It's just there, as an ambiguous, ill-defined notion rather than a tangible, measurable objective. There is no formula by which to gauge how much of it you will need, and no familiar medical condition associated with the lack of it. It is the last of the four basic needs, and yet its first component, safety, actually has to be addressed before any of the other three. It may not even be a true need, certainly not in the way shelter, water, and food are. But in a true crisis, it could be the most important need of all for you and your loved ones, since its presence or absence may be the ultimate determinant in whether or not you survive. Depending on the nature of the crisis that you face, it may also be the most difficult one for you to provide.

The absolute safest place to be in your home when a disaster strikes is in the basement and as far away from windows as possible. If you don't have access to a basement then seek shelter in your bathroom, so long as it doesn't have any windows. Make sure to close all doors within the home as well. Wherever you plan to convene your family in an emergency, remember to store a bag filled with supplies to keep you going in that room. In addition to food and water, ensure that your bag has an appropriate amount of medical supplies as well.

Safe, as used here, means free from immediate physical danger. The room in which you are trapped is intact, and it is not collapsing on you. The house is not under water with you still inside of it. You're not in a bus that's careening down a mountainside. No one is shooting at you. In other words, as best you can tell, nobody and nothing is about to inflict harm on you. If you have already confronted an immediate danger or it has confronted you, whether a ferocious storm or a human being out to do evil upon you, you have successfully gotten beyond it and are now in a place free of that danger. In a sense, it is your perception of being safe more than anything else. An undetected asteroid way up in space may be aimed right at your front door, but if you don't know about it, for purposes of this discussion, you are safe, because you feel safe.

That perception of your circumstances is important, because it will very much determine your state of mind for responding to the greater crisis. Safe also means panic-free. If panic is likely to show itself at any point in a crisis, it is when you face immediate danger. Panic was designed for just such moments. It takes an enormous amount of conscious effort and will power to keep it in check, and there is no sure way to prepare yourself for it. You could employ the common practice of simply saying out loud to yourself, over and over, "Don't panic…. Don't panic…." It may actually help.

Ultimately, in the moment of danger, you can only do the best that you can to save yourself; and like yourself, you also have to do the best you can to get your mind to a place of safety. In fact, you need to do that before you can do anything else. If you're the head of the household, your family may look to you for assurance as well, and that can end up being a lot of pressure on your shoulders. However, it's an essential part of getting your family through a crisis unscathed. The number one way to instill a feeling of safety in your family, no matter what the situation, is to reassure them that everything is going to be fine. Simply stating that is not enough, though; you, yourself, have to stay calm and confident, and trust in the plan you've put in

Essential Items For Any First Aid Medical Kit

Having these basics on hand will help you deal with most general medical issues that you'll come across in an emergency:

- Adhesive cloth tape
- Non-latex gloves
- Roller bandages
- Sterile gauze
- Space blanket
- Oral thermometer
- Tweezers
- Scissors
- Compress dressings
- Adhesive bandages
- Ready-to-use tourniquet
- Pain reliever
- Fever reducer
- Blood clotting agents
- Antiseptic hand cleanser
- Alcohol wipes
- Hydrogen peroxide
- Instant cold packs

5 Quick Tips That Can Save Your Life

1. If you wake up in the middle of the night to hear all your taps outside running or what you think is a burst pipe, DO NOT GO OUT TO INVESTIGATE! These people turn on all your outside faucets full blast so that you will go out to investigate and then attack. This was mentioned on America's Most Wanted when they profiled the serial killer in Louisiana.

2. If a robber asks for your wallet and/or purse, DO NOT HAND IT TO HIM. Toss it away from you.... Chances are that he is more interested in your wallet and/or purse than you, and he will go for the wallet/purse. RUN LIKE MAD IN THE OTHER DIRECTION!

3. If you are ever thrown into the trunk of a car, kick out the back tail lights and stick your arm out the hole and start waving like crazy. The driver won't see you, but everybody else will. This has saved lives.

4. If someone is in the car with a gun to your head DO NOT DRIVE OFF. Instead gun the engine and speed into anything while simultaneously trying to get your seat belt on. This will most likely wreck your car, but your seat belt and air bag will save you. If the person is in the back seat they will get the worst of it. As soon as the car crashes bail out and run. It is better than having them find your body in a remote location.

5. If, especially at rest stops, a stranger comes up to your window and taps on it, DO NOT ROLL THE WINDOW DOWN ALL THE WAY!

6. Only roll the window down barely enough for them to hear you, and assertively tell the stranger to take a step back. Remember to rely heavily on your instincts; if it doesn't feel right, don't even bother speaking to them and drive away before any harm can be done.

place for just such an occasion. This will make it much easier on both you and your family members, and will help in keeping everyone's morale up when things look bleak.

As mentioned in the Introduction, not every crisis will necessarily bring with it a threat to you of immediate danger. It may impact your life suddenly, like a catastrophic collapse of the power grid or a worldwide economic crash might, but it won't necessarily present itself as an immediate, personal danger to you, one calling for a prompt and decisive (and panic-free) move to safety. Instead, life as you know it will tend to deconstruct incrementally, over time. In such a scenario, the survival plan that you've been formulating as you have read through these chapters will probably take shape in the same way.

Rather than in a fixed moment of time, when you catch your breath, consciously calm yourself, and then methodically assess your needs and determine how you will provide for them, you may do this in a series of lesser moments, likewise spread out over time, in a process that is more organic and subtle.

Once again, how events play out locally for you in any disaster scenario is impossible to predict, but serious weather and other natural events are more likely to bring an immediate threat to you; the same with war, or a sudden societal collapse that quickly leads to a war-like state of general, chaotic lawlessness. In these circumstances, your first and only objective is to get to a place that is free of any perceived immediate danger to you. Only then, when safe, can you move ahead with formulating and implementing your survival plan. So in a flash flood you go for the high ground; in a tornado you go low. In a war-like environment, where in essence your fellow human beings are the threat, you try your best to get to somewhere—anywhere—that is out of harm's way. In the darkest of scenarios, in the darkest of times, there may be no such place. In such circumstances, if you are to survive them, your only alternative may be to remove the threat. That is the most difficult choice of all that you or anyone else will be called upon to make in a crisis situation. In the process of preparing yourself in advance of it, that choice deserves your deepest, most careful, and most soul-searching reflection and discussion.

Free Life Saving Mobile App: Circle of 6

Perhaps the best violence-preventing app ever created is called Circle of 6 and it's entirely free. It's specifically made to get immediate help for a number of dangerous situations. Have a bad feeling? Lost? Being followed? With the touch of a button you can send a text message and your exact location to friends, family, or emergency personnel before you find yourself in a life-threatening situation. This app is highly recommended by MTV, Cosmopolitan, Tech Crunch, and many more, and won a technology innovation award from the White House. It's available for download at www.circleof6app.com

II: Is it Secure?

Security, as it applies to your environment, means safe—and more—for the foreseeable future. Your house is not going to fall down around you any time soon, or burn down in the wild fires that are expected to reach you in three days, or slide down the hillside when the blizzard snows melt. No animals (including humans) are going to wander into your residence in the middle of the night and harm you or eat all of

your food, because the windows are busted and the door won't lock. No one is going to kick you out of where you are, or try to take it away from you. You are out of the path of any dangers that you can reasonably foresee.

Secure also means that the environment you are in can continue to provide you with shelter, and with an adequate and uninterrupted supply of water and food. If your survival plan contemplates rescue, then it means that you are in a good place to signal from and be found (see more on Rescue, below). You should also have the ability to transport yourself away from this environment, should events occur or conditions arise that render it no longer safe and secure. Lastly, you should be able to communicate with the outside world in some way, so as to remain informed of events and conditions in your surrounding area that might impact you.

There are other elements you may consider important to you from a security standpoint as well. What you consider necessary may include the ability to stay connected with friends and relatives who are in other locations, or with a group, such as a religious community, that might also be widely scattered. You may feel that collective security efforts, shared with your neighbors, or other close engagement and activities with them from a community standpoint, are vital to your well being; or, you may feel that your privacy is most important to you. The ability to defend against attack from unwelcome visitors may be a concern for you, and arming yourself may be a top priority.

Once again, you have choices to make. The security of your environment for you and your family is ultimately your personal survival strategy. Take ownership of it now, in the preparation process, since you will decidedly own it when the time of crisis arrives.

III: How Safe and Secure?

What all of this discussion reveals is just how elusive and murky the notion of a safe and secure environment can be. It is the fourth of the essentials to be assessed and provided for in a crisis survival situation, but if it's that fuzzy, how essential can it be?

Hypothermia, dehydration, and starvation can each kill you; so sayeth the Rule of 3's. How much less than "safe and secure" is still survivable? The answer is: quite a bit.

Take the scenario presented at the end of Chapter One. That family was safe once the storm had passed and there were no perceivable immediate threats to their safety. But they were not in a secure environment. Their basic needs for shelter, food, and water were met, but only for the one- or two-day duration of the plan, until rescue arrived. They had no means of getting out if they needed to, and no ability to communicate with the outside world. So, how safe and secure was it? Enough to make a plan. Enough to survive. That is the ultimate measure of what constitutes a safe and secure environment: enough to get to next light. Each missing element may be considered necessary, but in an emergency you'll often figure out a way to survive without it.

When faced with a crisis, as you assess your first three basic needs, you must provide for them. A plan to stay out in the cold for the next two weeks and do nothing about the need for warmth is a plan to die. It's like a plan to go a week without water, or a month without food. But a plan that contemplates staying put in an environment that is less than fully safe and secure—a house without doors or windows to keep out animals at night, for example—can still be a plan to survive, if that's all you have to work with right now. You adapt, and you figure out a way to make it work until you can come up with something better. If it is an immediate threat to your safety that you face, your first and only choice is to stop it or get away from it; but a less than completely secure environment may still be the best environment for you to survive in.

IV: Preparing a Safe and Secure Environment

For some, this aspect of preparation is not just the most important aspect, it is the focal point of all efforts. It is the goal towards which the bulk of all energy and resources are aimed, and all efforts are concentrated. The primary gathering of knowledge consists of what's gleaned from doomsday websites or reality TV shows, featuring others of like mindset. However, this approach is misguided at best and dangerous at worst.

The best approach to the advance preparation of a safe and secure environment for you and your loved ones is to immerse yourself in as much reliable information as possible, as to all aspects of security, and then to choose what will likely work best for you. First, you must acknowledge a simple fact: No physical structure, no matter how deeply buried or how well hidden, no matter how off-grid or how well armed and armored, can withstand every conceivable threat and still provide you with a suitable environment in which to live. There is only one type of structure that comes even close. It's called a castle, and somebody figured out how to effectively storm one of those about 800 years ago. Today, you'd better also keep a close watch on the skies.

While you may prefer some type of concrete protection for your home, you don't have to go nearly that far. This simple plan will decrease the chances of your home being robbed dramatically: A burglar's main enemies are light, time, and noise. Having a motion detection light is a great deterrent for keeping away house burglars. Also, installing an extra deadbolt on your front door as well as making sure you lock all windows will do a world of good in changing a thief's mind about breaking in. For noise, simple door and window alarms will be the quickest way to alert you to a break in, as well as scare the criminal away. In the aftermath of a disaster, such as a hurricane or tornado, piling trash and debris around your home as if it has already been ransacked can help disguise your home and make it less attractive to potential looters.

No typical residence can effectively be rendered completely assault-proof, fireproof, bulletproof, and explosion-proof, regardless of the measures taken. For every door there is a battering ram; for every wall there is a trebuchet; for every moat there is a bridge. For every inch of armor plating added, there is something stronger that will penetrate it; for every additional measure of stopping power, there is something out there that won't be stopped. Beyond all that, nothing built is ever completely nature- proof.

Keeping the military off your back in times of a crisis can be a bit tricky, especially if you have stores of food that you're trying to keep hidden. The main factor in whether or not you'll be bothered by the government during an emergency situation is how you procured your food stockpile. If you didn't pay in cash, in person, then chances are that your food storage is known to others. This is something you want to avoid. You should do your best to always use cash and keep your name and the information of your purchases off of any type of data device which can be obtained by others.

Each individual measure you take adds to both your real level of security and to your sense of it, and for that reason should not be discounted or dismissed. If you feel that owning a firearm will help in that regard, it's important to learn how to handle one before you get into a situation where it may have to be used.

The steps you choose to take in advance to help secure your environment should focus first on protecting your other three essentials: shelter (particularly its ability to provide warmth), water, and food. If firewood or extra fuel canisters are stacked outside in the open, they will soon disappear. An obvious and unprotected hand pump affixed your private well can turn into a public watering hole for unwelcome visitors. An unfenced, unattended-to garden is an invitation to browse. The nature of the community in which you live—rural, semi-urban, or densely populated and stacked high—will very much dictate the type and the extent of the measures that you can reasonably take. It will also dictate how effective they will be. Let common sense, mixed in with a healthy dose of devil's advocacy, be your guide.

V: Staying Connected in an Emergency

After the three essentials, also concern yourself with communications and transportation. Cell phones are essential. Even though they may not be operable or last for very long following the onset of a crisis, they are still the most effective and versatile communications option available today. A backup phone on a different network than your primary phone may increase your chances of receiving a signal when one carrier goes down or becomes congested. A traditional land-line phone is a more reliable alternative to a second cell phone, but cannot be taken with you if you have to flee your home. At about $80, the SpareOne emergency phone is a popular

and affordable model that can also double as a flashlight and emits an audio alert: www.spareone.com

The best way for you to stay informed, even if you have no power is by using a hand cranked radio. These are absolutely essential to have during an extended crisis, and happen to be quite affordable as well. If you don't happen to have one on hand, then using a simple and inexpensive radio that runs off of batteries is your next option. These basic AM radios tend to use batteries at a slow rate and tend to be highly portable. If you do plan to use this type of radio, make sure you have plenty of back up batteries for it. It would also be wise to have back up radios as well, just in case your primary one gets wet or damaged.Battery-powered receivers will last as long as your supply of batteries holds out and the hand crank-powered models will last for as long as your wrist holds out. Here again, having more than one means of receiving information from the outside world is the best option. An easy, inexpensive means of communicating amongst yourselves more locally in an emergency is a whistle around every neck, along with an agreed-upon set of signals for everyone in your makeshift network.

As to transportation, roads may or may not be passable or even open following a crisis. Public transportation may be one of the first services to come to a halt. Travel may itself be dangerous, particularly if a state of lawlessness exists. If you need to get out of your area fast or to get somewhere else, a vehicle will still be your best option, however. Keep it garaged or in some other secure location, keep it maintained, and keep it fueled. It will do you no good if it's stripped, stolen, or on empty. A bicycle for each family member is your best second option.

A word about energy. Going off-grid to any extent, via solar, bio-fuel, or some other alternative to reliance on traditional energy sources is becoming much more achievable and affordable, so you should investigate it seriously. You should also seriously investigate the implementation of strict energy conservation practices. In a survival situation, available energy in any form is not a luxury, it's a necessity. It warms you, it purifies your water, and it prepares your food. It also does your work. Whether derived from the sun, a tree, or a container of fuel, or residing within the muscles of your own arms and legs, energy can spell the difference between living and dying. It is a valuable commodity, and it should be treated as such.

VI: Firearms For Home Protection

There are a multitude of factors to take into consideration when choosing an appropriate gun for home defense. For example, are you single or do you have a family? If you have children, or even friends or relatives that might stay with you in times of crisis, then purchasing an appropriate gun safe is essential to keep the weapon out of untrained hands. If you're single, with no roommates, then you'll find the decision making process a bit more simplified.

The first thing you'll want to do is find something that suits you. You might have a friend who constantly brags about his Smith & Wesson 357 Magnum revolver and how it's the perfect pistol, but what's perfect for him may not be a good choice for you. Go to a local gun shop and check out different models, taking note of which ones feel good in your hands. Some essentials that you'll want to keep in mind are:

- **Grip size** - Does your hand fit around it comfortably enough for you to be able to reach the trigger and safety without straining?

- Ambidextrous safety - If you are left handed, will you still be able flip the safety off? (NOTE: Safeties come in a wide variety and not all work the same.)

- Caliber - Is the gun in a caliber that is both large enough to get the job done and small enough for you to shoot confidently? You may not know the answer to these until you find the opportunity to go shooting with a knowledgeable friend or professional instructor.

- Price - "You get what you pay for" is a very common phrase and it is especially relevant when deciding on a gun. If you're working with a tight budget, you may find it in your best interest to hold off on buying a gun until you have enough cash to spend on a quality weapon.

Deciding on a type of gun for home defense may be more complicated than you had anticipated. The main types of guns are shotguns, rifles, and pistols. All of these are divided into two main categories; semi-automatic and action firearms. Actions are largely comprised of single action (pistols), pump action (shotguns), bolt action, and lever action (rifles). Action-based firearms require manually performed steps in order to load a round into the chamber.

Semi-automatics, also known as auto loaders, do not require additional steps between trigger pulls in order for the firearm to discharge multiple rounds. Arguments have been made that the semi auto is a better option for home defense because they enable you to fire rounds in quicker succession at an assailant. They are, however, inherently more dangerous to a novice gun owner who has not had formal training.

Each type of gun has advantages and disadvantages that you must be aware of before you can decide which type will work for you:

- Shotguns - These will usually possess the largest amount of firepower, meaning that one up close direct hit will be more than enough to stop an assailant, no matter how big. Unfortunately, one of the major downsides to a shotgun is that they drastically lose effectiveness at longer ranges. They also have a low amount of accuracy. The brands that may interest you are Mossberg, Benelli, Beretta, Remington, and Saiga.

- Rifles - These will provide the highest amount of accuracy at any range and come in a wide variety of firepower. They tend to have lower mobility and can become awkward to deploy in close quarter combat scenarios. They also are more at risk of causing collateral damage, if a round strays or goes entirely through an assailant. Remington, Colt, FN, Bushmaster, and Smith & Wesson are a few high quality rifle makers. (NOTE: You should always be aware of what is behind and around your target.)

Pistols -These are the highest in mobility and are largely popular because they are so easy to conceal.
They have a moderate amount of accuracy. Like a shotgun, they drastically lose effectiveness at longer ranges. They usually have the least amount of firepower as well. Popular brands include Beretta, Kimber, Sig Sauer, Colt, Ruger, and Glock.

If you have no prior firearms training or experience, then this is the next thing you'll want to obtain. Professional firearms instructors are readily available in most areas. You can usually find an NRA instructor or coach. Otherwise, some police departments offer firearms safety courses as well. If you're not sure where to find training, you can start by asking around at your nearest firing range. The same goes if you wish to obtain a conceal carry permit.

No matter what you decide on, it is imperative that you use the utmost care and precaution when dealing with firearms. It's also just as important that you teach your family the importance of handling firearms properly. Ensure that all guns are out of reach from small children at all times. Remember, safety first.

VII: How To Survive a Riot

In a crisis situation, where everyone around you is embracing chaos and madness, you have to stay calm and think clearly in order to keep you and your loved ones safe. Riots are generally prefaced with plenty of warning time. Usually the current political climate, social media chatter, and local news will be enough to keep anyone informed enough to predict when a riot will occur. However, you may find yourself in the middle of riot nevertheless.

If you become embroiled with an angry mob, you must keep these tips in mind to help you get through the ordeal safely:

- Stay calm - Your mindset is going to be the main factor in whether you get your family out of this situation. You won't do anyone any good if you're not successful in overcoming anxiety issues and stress. If you are able to remain calm, you'll find that you will be able to think much more clearly. You'll be able to take note of your surroundings while not being distracted by them.

- Don't stick out - The last thing you want to is gain the attention of rioters. If you are wearing any type of clothing that makes you look like military or police, take it off and throw it away immediately.

You also don't want to look like a rioter, and have the police treat you like one. In order to avoid this mistake, you must avoid the larger groups as you continue away from the danger.

- Avoid the situation - You'll want to get out of the area ASAP. Once a riot starts, there's no telling whether it'll dissipate or turn into a major crisis. Your best bet is to bug out. If you have a vehicle nearby, you'll want to get to it quickly. Do not attract attention by running,

- just walk quickly to your car or truck and get in. Once in the vehicle, lock your doors, and drive away. Do not speed off, just drive normal and avoid high traffic areas. If you're stuck on foot, then quickly find a less travelled road and proceed in that direction.

- Go Indoors - If you can't find a safe exit strategy, then the next best thing is to go inside one of the buildings. The majority of the violence from a riot will be on the streets and rarely will major chaos occur inside of a building, other than shops and stores getting trashed. Once you are inside of a building, go up a few floors so you can overlook the street. Giving yourself a vantage point will allow you to survey for possible escape routes.

- Keep your ear to the ground - Even if you make it away from the riot's inception point, you may not be out of trouble yet. Keep checking social media and news for further updates. If the riot continues growing, then you may want to consider leaving your home and getting out of the city while the authorities try to regain control. Staying informed will be one of your biggest allies in this type of situation, so never underestimate the importance of a hand-cranked radio.

5 Essential Drills To Keep Your Family Safe

Preparing your family for a disaster scenario could save the lives of your loved ones. It's important that your family knows what to do in case of one of these emergencies. Doing drills for common scenarios goes a long ways towards being prepared for the worst.

In any situation you should have some basic items that are easily accessible; a bug out bag already stocked with essential items and a medical emergency kit will cover most of your needs. Here are five basic drills to help keep your family safe:

Tornado Drill

Before you are ready to conduct a tornado drill, there are a few things that you'll need to work out. First, you'll want to figure out what the safest location is in your home, and the quickest route to get there. Once you have this figured out, you'll need to ensure that there are never any obstructions; make a rule  that no toys can be laying in that area. You don't want to find yourself tripping over things if the power goes out.

- Gather family and emergency items (bug out bag & medkit)

- Avoid all windows and get to safe area.

- Get under a sturdy table or cover everyone with thick padding.

- Stay put until you are certain there is no more danger.

Fire Drill

First, you'll need to make sure your house is equipped with multiple smoke detectors as well as fire extinguishers. Next, you'll want to have at least two escape routes planned. One will serve as your primary route, and the second will be an alternative route in case the first one is blocked. Obviously you'll want the the alternative to be in the opposite direction as the primary in order to steer clear of the fire. Lastly, you'll want to pick a rendezvous location outside of the home; most likely this will be directly across the street from the front of your home.

- Gather family and grab emergency items (bug out bag & medkit)

- Proceed to primary escape route.

- If blocked, proceed to alternative route.

- Continue to meet location.

- Once you are certain everyone is safe, call 911.

Hurricane Drill

In this scenario, you'll want to be familiar with roads leaving your area. You'll also want to have a pre-determined friend or relative that you can stay with in case of such a disaster. Hurricanes generally allow you far more time to pack essential items and fuel your vehicle in advance of its approach. If you are not ordered to evacuate, follow the tornado drill. If you are, follow this one.

- Gather family and emergency items (bug out bag & medkit)

- Pack enough food and supplies to last at least three days.

- Leave as soon as the evacuation is ordered.

- Call out of state friend/relative and give an estimation of your arrival.

- Do your best to avoid flooded roads, fallen trees, and bottled traffic spots.

- Keep checking in with your friend/relative until you've arrived.

Flood Drill

 This may be similar to the hurricane drill, since it is very common for severe floods to require evacuations. If that is the case, follow the hurricane drill. Otherwise, follow this drill. If you live in an area that is prone to flooding, it is wise to have a life jacket for every member of your family. Owning a canoe is probably in your best interest as well.

- Remove any valuable items from the basement.

- Shut off utilities.

- Gather your family and emergency items (bug out bag, medkit, and floatation items)

- Go to the top floor.

- Listen to emergency channels on your radio.

Burglary Drill

You rarely hear of families practicing break-in drills, but these can be just as important as natural disaster drills. For this drill, it is assumed that you have a firearm or other self-defense weapon in your home. Steer away from using knives, other than as a last resort. While knives are extremely deadly in the right hands, they require that you get up close to an assailant in order to attack. If you don't have a gun, opt for a bat, golf club, or something else that gives you the advantage of being able to keep out of arm's reach while still being able to deal deadly strikes.

During a break-in, the safest place to go is the room that is farthest from any entrances to the house. If your home has multiple floors, then go upstairs and as far away from the stairwell as possible. Make sure that you have a defensive weapon waiting for you in this room.

(NOTE: If a family member gets held hostage before you can get to them, do not try to attack the burglar. It's better for you to let them take your possessions than entice them into harming a loved one. Do what they ask and be as cooperative as possible.)

- Quickly gather your family and hurry them to the safe area.

- Once everyone is inside, lock the door.

- Barricade the door with a large piece of furniture.

- Put your children in a closet or under a bed and call 911.

- Do not let anything through the door until you are certain the police have cleared the home.

Obviously, during these drills, you won't actually be calling 911 or following through with some of the courses of action. You want to make them as realistic as possible, so it is up to you how far you want to go in preparation. It is recommended that you actually go through each step as best as possible. When practice makes perfect, you'll appreciate these drills in a crisis situation. Hope for the best, prepare for the worst.

VIII: The Entire Survival Plan

You now have the basic knowledge you need for smart, competent advance preparation for a crisis. You also have a survival plan, one which you will implement when a crisis arrives. One more review of this plan:

● Before anything else, you will make sure that you are not in danger; that you are in a safe place, both physically and mentally.

● Calmly, and without panic, you will assess your three basic needs, those being, in order, **shelter, water,** and **food,** by applying the **Rule of 3's.** You will determine whether you can you immediately provide for each of them in the short term.

● If you cannot immediately provide for each of them, you will determine which of them is the most pressing, in terms of time, and what you have to do to in order to provide for that need in the short term.

● Once you have determined what you need to do in order to provide for those three needs in the short term, you will carry out the necessary tasks.

● You will also assess your surroundings and determine whether you are in **a safe and secure environment**. If not, you will determine what you can do to make it so, and you will do it, or you will find another place that is better. In doing this, you will also make an assessment of your future, long-term basic needs of **shelter, water,** and **food**.

Every step you take from this point forward will be aimed at better facilitating the implementation of this plan when crisis does arrive.

IX: Next Light

How far into the future do you plan? A week? Six months? Forever? Or is it just two or three days, until rescue arrives? You might think farther out is always better, but that isn't so, particularly when the crisis you face is more immediate and the problems that it presents are more difficult for you to deal with. The danger of planning too far ahead in a survival situation is the risk of failure. This is the psychology of survival.

In crisis, you are in difficult times. The farther out you reach, the greater the likelihood that you will encounter obstacles and unanticipated events along the way that will undermine all of your planning. Long before you get close to the end objective you've chosen, you are burdened by your failures and left with a plan that simply doesn't work. In difficult times, that sense of failure will take you to a very dark place, one where you feel that you may as well have had no plan at all. You may as well give up. This is where the concept of **Next Light** comes into play.

In Chapter Two there is mentioned some results from the studies of real-life stories of survival. A common thread found in them was that many of those who survived challenging, sometimes extreme conditions did so because they had a plan to continue living. Another common thread, though, was that if the plan pushed too far out into the future, or it aimed for too ambitious an objective, it was less likely to succeed. With the resultant sense of failure came a loss of the will to live.

But even in those situations, if the people involved were able to rein in their objectives and re-direct their aims towards a series of shorter, more achievable goals, their chances of survival increased once again. For a group of sailors in a lifeboat on a storm-ravaged sea, their initial plan looked to their ultimate objective, which was to find land. The plan that ultimately worked for them was to keep bailing water until morning. That is **Next Light.**

In your preparation for crisis, you may choose six months as your objective. You now have the knowledge, so you gather your resources and you prepare yourself and your family accordingly. It's a long enough time, in your view, for life to return to some level of normalcy following a major upheaval, and it's entirely reasonable. Or, you may choose a month instead, if only for budgetary reasons. You may choose to bug out to a cabin in the woods forever. Or, you may simply decide to turn your spare bedroom in the basement into a tornado shelter.

It's your decision. Regardless of what you decide, keep in mind that when crisis does arrive your first objective may end up being completely outside the scope of what you were expecting. At that point, you may find that your only objective is to make it two weeks without freezing to death. That becomes the "How far?" of your survival plan. You aim for two weeks because, given the circumstances, it's achievable. It has to be, and you have to make it so, with determination and with clever adaptation, otherwise you die. It's your **Next Light**. After two weeks (or sooner if necessary or advantageous) you formulate a new plan based on your then-circumstances, a plan with a new objective and another **Next Light**. After that, you do it again. Throughout the process, you constantly adapt. And you get better at it. And you succeed.

When crisis does arrive you will be prepared, and you will always have a plan. You will choose your objectives carefully and realistically, while looking no further into the future than where you can see Next Light. Eventually normalcy has to return. If it doesn't, a new normal of some kind will prevail. Eventually you'll be able to cast your gaze out farther, until the light is constant for as far as you can see. At that point you will have survived.

ADVANCED SURVIVAL TRAINING

Keeping up with world events and the changing political climate is imperative if you want to stay vigilant in your preparations. Likewise, having access to ongoing, advanced training will give you the survival edge when disaster strikes. In order to stay up-to-date with current events, learn about the latest disaster preparation trends, and receive new training videos each week that walk you step-by- step through dozens of life-saving survival topics, you'll need to become a member of the United Survivalists Association (U.S.A.). This organization is a one-of-a-kind resource for news and information that you can't get anywhere else, and it's only available to you as an owner of Alive After Crisis. To claim your membership to the United Survivalists Association, visit: http:// aliveaftercrisis.com/members/u- s-a/

Review of Chapter Five

What have you learned in this Chapter?

- Safe means free from immediate physical danger

- You must first be safe, physically and mentally, before you can do anything else.

- A secure environment is one that is safe for the foreseeable future and will provide you with adequate shelter, water, and food.

- You now have a survival plan.

- In a crisis, your survival plan should look no further than Next Light.

What is your plan at this point?

Other topics to consider and to discuss with others:

1. What are the details of your security plan?

2. What provision have you made for communications?

3. What provision have you made for alternative energy?

List of Items for Preparation

1. Batteries.

1. Cell phones.

3. Solar battery chargers.

4. Emergency radios.

5. Medical kit.

6. Automobile maintenance supplies.

7. Bicycles.

8. Security weapons.

Preparation: A Conversation

Question: This is an interesting approach to disaster preparation, but there aren't a lot of details in it. How exactly do I start preparing?

Answer: You already have. You read Next Light. You have a survival plan now, and that's an excellent start. What you're really asking is what's next.

Question: Okay, then, what's next?

Answer: That's really up to you, but let's see if I can help you along. Take any object in this room, say the light bulb in the lamp sitting next to you. Assume it's the only bulb you own right now. Will you need it in a crisis? Asked another way, will it serve any of your four basic human needs in a crisis?

Question: Shelter, no. Water and food, definitely not. Wait. On shelter, I suppose a light bulb could provide some warmth, but I can think of many better ways to do that.

Answer: Describe them.

Question: Well, there's always the furnace. If we still have power, we're all set. If not, there's a fireplace in my home. I'll need a bigger supply of firewood, though. I suppose I could keep it next to the shed, out of sight from the street. I'll also need to sit down and figure out how much more of it I'll need, especially if we have to boil drinking water and cook meals. How long should I plan for?

Answer: Choose your next light. You're in the very preliminary stages of preparation, so for now you can make it something arbitrary, say a month. You can always adjust it later, after you've better informed yourself and made more decisions on things.

Question: A month it is. I better start keeping notes. Back to shelter. I should make sure I have a sleeping bag for everybody in the family. Plus a couple of extras, in case we end up with company. Better check the supply of blankets, too. What if the house is destroyed though? I suppose I could make arrangements in advance to stay with my brother and his family in an emergency. Make it a mutual thing, cover each other. Better have a tent, too, in case we have trouble getting there. Hey, what's doing all this going to cost me?

Answer: What will it cost you if you don't do it?

Question: Yeah, point made. Shelter...shelter...space blankets! I should get a bunch of those, keep some in the car, too. What else?

Answer: Back to the light bulb. Your fourth basic need.

Question: A safe and secure environment. A light bulb doesn't make me any safer. It does provide light, though, and that could provide some security at night. Assuming we still have power.

Answer: If not?

Question: If not, there's candles, and flashlights, even those little solar-powered outdoor lights. I could also look into going solar on the house. Of course, if I'm the only house on the block with it, and I'm the only one with lights on at night, now I have a potential security problem. I need to think about that, too. This gets pretty complicated, doesn't it?

Answer: It feels that way at first, which is why some people stop before they get very far with it. But don't let the apparent size of the task fool you. Most of it is still uncharted territory for you, so it looks a lot bigger than it really is. Stick with it. Things level out and get more manageable fairly quickly. So, what's your decision on the light bulb? Do you need it?

Question: If I really look at it, I guess I don't. At least I know that I can easily get by without it. So, cross one light bulb off the list?

Answer: You might want to hold onto that one. You just built a very nice start to your preparation plan around it.

Question: A light bulb. What a great idea.